BERMUDA GUIDE 2024

Discover Pristine Beaches and Hidden Treasures | Adventure, Relaxation, Culture, and Hotels"

Rita R. Nowlin

Table of Content

CHAPTER 1: INTRODUCTION TO BERMUDA

Welcome To Bermuda

As I stepped foot on the magnificent island of Bermuda, the green seas swirled elegantly, hugging the coastline. I felt an unexplained excitement racing through me as my jet dropped, an eagerness for the wonders that awaited me in this paradisiacal land.

A symphony of hues met me as I stepped into the silky pink sands of Horseshoe Bay -

cerulean waters blending flawlessly with the azure sky, producing a composition so exquisite that it appeared snatched from the realms of magic. The warm wind brought a delicate aroma of salt and adventure, luring me to explore every nook and corner of this enthralling Atlantic jewel.

I couldn't help but be intrigued by the island's distinct combination of British refinement and island vivacity as I wandered through the winding alleys lined with pastel-colored homes, each oozing its own charm. The rhythmic beats of Gombey drums boomed through the streets, filling the air with an enticing energy and inviting me to participate in the vivid celebration of Bermudian culture.

The lush greenery moved in unison, whispering stories of Bermuda's rich past - tales of daring explorers, famous shipwrecks, and secret treasures waiting to be discovered beneath the clear seas. The supernatural attraction of the island appeared to reverberate in every coral reef and towering limestone formation, compelling me to dive further into its mysteries.

I was captivated by the ethereal beauty of this corner of paradise as the day gave way to a flaming sunset, sending hues of amber and gold across the horizon. It was more than simply a vacation; it was an immersion into a world where time appeared to slow down, enabling one to savour every moment, sensation, and stunning panorama that Bermuda so generously provided.

With a wanderlust in my heart and a spirit aroused by the island's beauty, I knew my voyage had only just begun, promising days packed with adventures to come in this sanctuary of calm and wonder - Bermuda, a diamond glittering amidst the cerulean vastness of the Atlantic Ocean.

Geographical Overview

Bermuda, while being frequently referred to as a single island, is actually an archipelago comprising around 138 islands and islets located in the North Atlantic Ocean. Bermuda is famed for its enticing pink-sand beaches, crystal-clear turquoise seas, and spectacular coral reefs. It is located around 650 miles off the coast of North Carolina, USA.

The main island, generally referred to as Main Island or simply Bermuda, is home to the majority of the people. Bermuda has a highly diversified terrain despite its tiny size (approximately 21 square miles). Bermuda's topography is both gorgeous and diverse, ranging from stunning limestone cliffs to lush tropical flora and calm, hidden bays.

The islands are the visible peaks of a submerged volcanic mountain range, and their unusual creation adds to Bermuda's unique geology. The distinctive pink sand on Bermuda's beaches is a result of red foraminifera, microscopic marine invertebrates that generate a crimson pigment on coral reefs.

Bermuda's prominent sights include the breathtaking Horseshoe Bay Beach, the enigmatic Crystal Caves with their intricate formations, and historic monuments such as the Town of St. George, a UNESCO World Heritage Site that provides an insight into the island's colonial past.

Bermuda's geology includes more than simply its land structures; it also has a lively undersea ecosystem. The surrounding water is teeming with marine life, making it a snorkelling and diving paradise. The Bermuda Triangle, famous for its mysterious disappearances, adds to the region's already interesting geological composition.

History And Culture

History:

Bermuda's history is a rich tapestry of exploration, colonisation, and resistance. The islands were discovered in the early 16th century by Spanish explorer Juan de Bermdez and later inhabited by the English in the early 17th century. The island's architecture reflects this colonial tradition, with pastel-colored buildings and beautiful cottages reflecting British influence.

The UNESCO World Heritage Site of St. George is a living testimony to Bermuda's colonial heritage. Its winding lanes, mediaeval forts, and centuries-old structures tell stories of pirates, commerce, and maritime dominance.

Furthermore, Bermuda's history is entwined with stories of slavery, abolition, and African descendants' contributions. Visiting the Tucker House Museum and the National Museum of Bermuda gives insight on the island's complicated socioeconomic past, demonstrating the island's resiliency and cultural diversity.

Culture:

Bermuda's culture is a lively tapestry created by a blend of European, African, and Caribbean elements. The island's Gombey culture, which consists of colourful and rhythmic dance performances accompanied by drumming and complex costumes, honours the island's African origin.

Traditions like as the Gombey Festival, Cup Match cricket, and the yearly Bermuda International Film Festival bring people and visitors together to celebrate art, sports, and cultural variety.

Cuisine, which combines British, African, and Caribbean flavours, is another important aspect of Bermudian culture. To taste the island's gastronomic heritage, try fish chowder, Bermuda fish sandwich, and cassava pie. The legendary Dark 'n Stormy drink, created with Bermuda's own Gosling's Black Seal Rum, and the local rum cake are must-tries for a taste of true Bermudian flavours.

Bermuda now cherishes its legacy while also embracing new influences, as seen by its booming art scene, music festivals, and a thriving gastronomic environment. Exploring local art galleries, witnessing live music performances, or participating in cultural festivals allows visitors to get firsthand knowledge of Bermuda's vibrant and growing cultural character.

Climate And Best Time To Visit

Seasonal Changes:

Spring (March to May): This season heralds the rebirth of Bermuda's vivid vegetation and is an ideal time to visit due to temperate weather and less visitors. It's perfect for outdoor activities like hiking and discovering the natural beauty of the island.

Summer (June to August): Temperatures average in the upper 80s Fahrenheit (about 30°C) throughout these months. It's peak tourist season because of the beautiful beach weather, which is ideal for swimming, snorkelling, and other water activities. During this period, expect more people and higher hotel costs.

Autumn (September to November): As the summer crowds go, autumn in Bermuda brings comfortable temps and calmer beaches. It's a great time to go diving since the water is still warm, and you could see some interesting marine species.

Winter (December to February): While temperatures drop in the winter, Bermuda stays quite pleasant in comparison to many other places. Daytime highs are approximately 70°F (21°C), making it an ideal winter getaway from harsher regions. It's a slower season for tourism, with reduced prices and an opportunity to get a closer look at local life.

When is the best time to visit:

The ideal time to visit Bermuda is determined primarily by personal tastes and preferred activities. Summer is the ideal season for beachgoers and those looking for aquatic activities. Spring and fall, on the other hand, may be ideal for a more leisurely and cost-effective trip with lovely weather. Winter, while chilly, still provides a pleasant island experience away from the tourists.

Remember that Bermuda's position in the Atlantic Ocean renders it vulnerable to storms from June to November. While direct impacts are uncommon, it is prudent to monitor weather forecasts at this time.

Overall, Bermuda provides something unique all year long, appealing to a wide range of interests and preferences, ensuring that tourists may enjoy its beauty and activities regardless of the season.

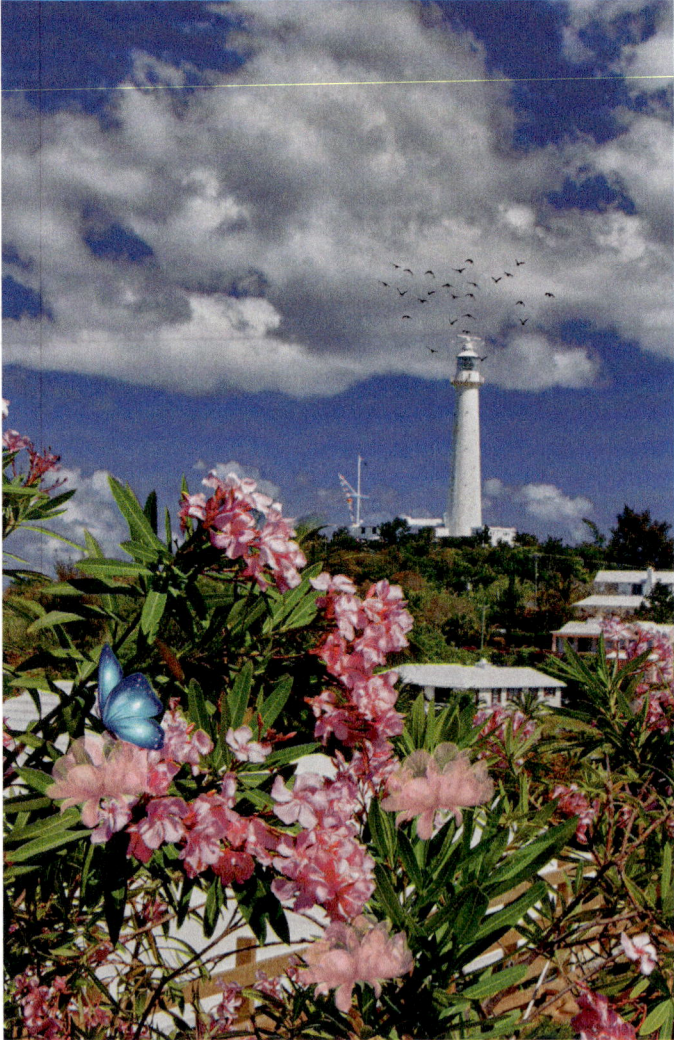

CHAPTER 2: GETTING TO BERMUDA

Transportation Options

Transportation via Public:

Buses: The pink buses of Bermuda provide an efficient and cost-effective means to move between parishes and attractions. The bus network covers the majority of the island and runs throughout the day. Tokens or tickets for several rides can be purchased by visitors. Fares for a single journey range from $2.75 to $5, depending on the route and the passenger's age.

Ferries: The ferry system on the island connects several sites across the islands, providing scenic rides over the magnificent blue seas. Ferries connect Hamilton (the capital), the Royal Naval Dockyard, and other vital areas, offering a pleasurable and picturesque mode of transportation. Ferry costs for a one-way trip starts at about $20 and might vary based on distance and time of day.

Twizy and Scooters:For many tourists, renting scooters or Twizy is a popular option. These cars are available from a variety of rental firms around the island, allowing the freedom and convenience to explore Bermuda at one's own leisure. However, it is critical to follow local traffic regulations and safety requirements.

Scooter rentals start about $50 per day while Twizy rentals start around $80 per day.

Taxis:Taxis are common across Bermuda and provide a comfortable and convenient means of transportation. Taxis are available at authorised stands, hotels, and tourist sites. It is best to confirm prices before embarking on your travel, since costs may fluctuate. The first mile costs roughly $8, and each extra mile costs $3. Late-night and Sunday rates are also subject to surcharges.

Rental cars: Bermuda has a severe limit on the number of rental cars available. To borrow a car, visitors must first apply for a temporary driver's licence. While this choice provides flexibility, keep in mind that Bermuda drives on the left side of the road.

Walking and cycling: Because of Bermuda's small size and gorgeous terrain, walking and cycling are popular ways to explore particular locations. Many hotels provide bicycle rentals, and there are dedicated pathways and trails for cyclists.

Using these transit choices to navigate Bermuda allows visitors to see the island's beauty and attractions while catering to different tastes and comfort levels.

Entry Requirements And Visa Information

Most nationals do not need a visa to visit Bermuda for up to 90 days. All visitors must, however, fulfil a few admission criteria.

Passport

All travellers to Bermuda must have a passport that is valid for at least six months beyond their intended departure date. In addition, the passport must include at least one vacant page for the admission stamp.

Return or onward travel ticket

All guests are also required to provide confirmation of onward or return travel, such as a confirmed airline ticket or cruise itinerary. This is done to demonstrate to the immigration official that you do not plan to immigrate to Bermuda.

Evidence of ample finances

Visitors must also be able to demonstrate that they have enough money to maintain themselves throughout their stay in Bermuda. This might be a bank statement, a credit card statement, or a traveler's check.

Form of Digital Arrival

Before arriving in Bermuda, all tourists must fill out a digital arrival form. The form may be completed online at the Bermuda Government website.

Certain Countries Must Meet Additional Requirements

To enter Bermuda, citizens of a few countries, notably China, India, and Sri Lanka, must hold a multi-reentry visa (MRV). The MRV can be obtained via your native country's British embassy or consulate.

Visa Guidelines

While most visitors to Bermuda are not needed to obtain a visa, there are a few exceptions. These are some examples:

Business travellers: If you want to remain in Bermuda for longer than 90 days, you may need a business visa.

Crew men on ships and aeroplanes may require a crew visa.

Students: Students who want to study in Bermuda for longer than six months may be required to get a student visa.

How to Obtain a Visa

Visa applications can be submitted online to the British Embassy or consulate in your native country. Because visa processing times vary, it is critical to apply well in advance of your trip plans.

Contact Information

Please contact the British Embassy or consulate in your native country for additional information on entrance procedures and visa requirements for Bermuda.

Airport And Port Information

Airport Specifics

Bermuda's only commercial airport is L.F. Wade International Airport (BDA). It is located on the island's east coast, approximately 10 miles (16 km) from the capital, Hamilton. There is one main terminal and two runways at the airport. The terminal is equipped with a number of stores, restaurants, and other services.

Bermuda is a major tourist destination, and the L.F. Wade International Airport serves flights from the United States, Canada, the United Kingdom, and Europe. There are also several charter airlines that fly to Bermuda.

Port Specifics

Hamilton Harbour and King's Wharf are Bermuda's two principal ports. Hamilton Harbour is the primary port for cruise ships and is located in the capital city of Hamilton. King's Wharf is a popular port for ferries and yachts on the west end of the island.

Both ports provide guests with a range of services such as stores, restaurants, and cafés. Taxis and buses are also available to carry people to and from the ports.

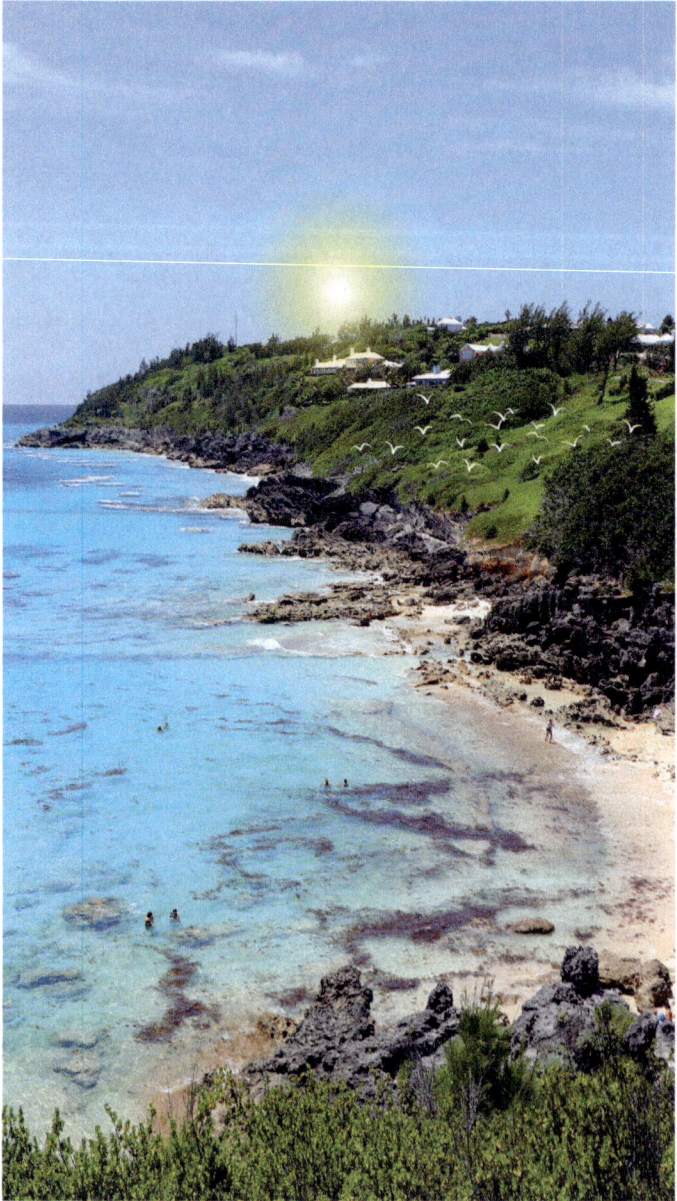

CHAPTER 3: ACCOMMODATION IN BERMUDA

Types Of Accommodation

- **Hotels And Resorts**

Rosewood Bermuda: Rosewood Bermuda is a magnificent beachside resort with 99 rooms, suites, and cottages. It is the pinnacle of luxury in Bermuda. Elegant decor, outstanding service, and world-class amenities make the resort an ideal choice for discriminating travellers. Two swimming pools, a spa, a fitness centre, and a range of water sports activities are available to guests. The nightly rate begins at $1,200.

The Reefs Resort & Club has been welcoming visitors to Bermuda for almost 60 years. With 199 rooms and suites facing the gorgeous South Shore, The Reefs provides a peaceful and luxury setting. Five swimming pools, a spa, a fitness centre, and a selection of restaurants and cafes are available to guests. The nightly rate begins at $800.

Hamilton Princess & Beach Club is located in the centre of Hamilton, Bermuda's capital city. With 400 rooms and suites, the Hamilton Princess combines modern and classic grandeur. Two swimming pools, a spa, a fitness centre, and a selection of restaurants and cafes are available to guests. The nightly rate begins at $600.

The Loren at Pink Beach: With only 48 rooms and suites, this compact beachside resort is ideal for getting away from the throng. The Loren features breathtaking views of Pink Beach, a world-class spa, and a range of water sports. The nightly rate begins at $1,000.

Cambridge Beaches Resort & Spa: This family-friendly resort sits on a beautiful peninsula on Bermuda's western coast. Cambridge Beaches has 125 rooms and suites, four pools, a spa, a fitness centre, and a number of restaurants and cafes. The nightly rate begins at $500.

Rosedon Hotel: Perched on a hilltop above Hamilton Sound, this historic jewel provides beautiful suites, a fine-dining restaurant, and breathtaking views. You should budget roughly $500 each night.

Royal Palms Hotel: Located in a 1903 structure, this tiny hotel offers cosy quarters, a restaurant and complimentary breakfast. It is also close to various beaches and tourist attractions. You should budget roughly $300 each night.

- **Bed And Breakfast**

Edgehill Manor Guest House: This magnificent bed & breakfast is located in Pembroke, Bermuda, only minutes from the ocean. It has spectacular ocean views and a range of facilities, such as a pool, a hot tub, and a tennis court. Prices begin at $200 per night.

Oxford House: This ancient bed & breakfast is located in St. George's, Bermuda, a UNESCO World Heritage Site. With vintage furniture and a pleasant environment, it provides a one-of-a-kind and unforgettable experience. Prices begin about $180 per night.

Kingston House B&B: Located in Pembroke, Bermuda, this adults-only bed and breakfast. It has a range of accommodations, including a honeymoon suite, as well as a lovely garden. Prices begin around $250 per night.

Watercolours: This bed and breakfast situated in a peaceful area of Southampton, Bermuda. It has cosy accommodations, a wonderful breakfast, and a welcoming staff. Prices begin around $120 per night.

Granaway Guest House & Cottages: This beautiful bed and breakfast is centrally located in Hamilton, Bermuda's capital city. It has a range of accommodations to choose from, including basic rooms, suites, and cottages. The

Granaway also features a lovely garden and a pool. Prices begin around $150 per night.

- **Vacation Rentals**

Apartments: Apartments are an excellent choice for budget-conscious travellers or couples. They usually have a kitchen, a living room, and one or two bedrooms. Prices start at $100

Houses: Because they provide greater room and privacy than apartments, houses are ideal for families or groups of friends. They usually have several bedrooms, a kitchen, a living room, and outside space. Prices start at $200

Villas: The most opulent sort of vacation rental, villas have huge rooms, private pools, and occasionally even staff. They are an excellent option for people looking to indulge on their holiday. Prices start at $500

Popular Areas To Stay

- **Hamilton:**

Hamilton is Bermuda's bustling capital, with a vibrant mix of culture, history, and modern facilities. Visitors may stay in a variety of lodgings, ranging from luxury hotels to boutique guesthouses. Fine dining restaurants, commercial districts, and cultural attractions such as the Bermuda National Gallery and historical sites abound throughout the city.

- **St. George's Cathedral:**

UNESCO World Heritage Site St. George's takes tourists back in time with its well-preserved colonial buildings and tiny cobblestone alleyways. There are delightful inns, bed-and-breakfasts, and guesthouses in this neighbourhood. It's ideal for people looking for a peaceful vacation while learning about Bermuda's history.

- **Southampton Parish**

Southampton Parish is home to some of the most stunning beaches on the island, including Horseshoe Bay Beach. Luxury resorts with spectacular ocean views, golf courses, and access to pink sand beaches suited for leisure and aquatic activities can be found here.

- **Warwick Parish**

Warwick Parish is well-known for its gorgeous coastline scenery and calm surroundings. Visitors may choose from a variety of lodging options, including hotels, resorts, and vacation rentals. Those looking for a more relaxed ambiance while yet being close to major attractions would enjoy the region.

- **Royal Naval Dockyard**

The Dockyard region, which is rich in nautical heritage, has a variety of lodging options, including hotels and vacation rentals. It serves as an entertainment area, including attractions such as the National Museum of Bermuda, shopping, restaurants, and water-based activities.

Where to stay in Bermuda is frequently determined by personal tastes, chosen activities, and the overall experience sought.

Budgeting And Booking Tips

- **Accommodation**:

Book Early: Book your lodgings early, especially during busy seasons, to obtain better rates and a greater range of alternatives.

Consider the following alternatives: Consider guesthouses, vacation rentals, or smaller hotels for potentially less expensive stays than larger resorts.

Off-Peak Travel: For reduced lodging prices, consider travelling during the shoulder seasons (spring or fall).

- **Modes of transportation:**

Passes for public transit: Purchase passes for buses and ferries, which provide inexpensive transportation around the island.

Scooter Rentals: While scooter rentals are handy, check scooter rental costs from several suppliers to discover reasonable pricing.

- **Eating**:

Local Eateries: Visit local restaurants and eateries for traditional Bermudian food at lower costs than fancy eating.

Consider hotels with kitchen facilities to make some meals and save money on dining out.

- **Extracurricular Activities:**

Attractions that are free or low-cost: Visit Bermuda's beaches, wildlife reserves, and free attractions such as historical sites or public parks.

Passes with Discounts: Look for passes with discounts on several attractions or activities.

- **Booking Suggestions:**

Flight and Hotel Packages: For possible savings, look for package offers that combine flights and lodgings.

Flexible trip Dates: Being flexible with trip dates allows for pricing comparisons at various periods, perhaps resulting in better offers.

Travel Deals and Alerts: To keep informed about discounts and deals, sign up for travel alerts or newsletters from airlines, hotels, or travel agents.

- **Payments and currency:**

Exchange Rates: Keep an eye on exchange rates so you may convert money at a good moment.

Credit Cards: Determine whether your credit card provides travel points or cashback on overseas transactions, which might save you money.

CHAPTER 4: EXPLORING BERMUDA'S REGION

Overview Of Different Parishes And Regions

Bermuda is split into nine parishes, each with its own distinct character and attractions. Exploring these parishes allows tourists to immerse themselves in the island's different landscapes, historical attractions, and cultural experiences.

1. Hamilton Parish:

Crystal Caves, a natural marvel with spectacular subterranean formations, may be seen here. Spittal Pond Nature Reserve, including scenic walking routes and chances for birding.

2. Smith's Parish:

The stunning John Smith's Bay Beach is famed for its pink sands. The Verdmont Historic House Museum exhibits Bermudian architecture and history.

3. Devonshire Parish:

Botanical Gardens, a tranquil haven with rich greenery and the unique Bermuda moongates. The Masterworks Museum of Bermuda Art exhibits both local and foreign artworks.

4. Pembroke Parish:

Bermuda's capital, Hamilton, is located here, and it is bustling with stores, restaurants, and cultural activities.

Victoria Park is a nice green park suitable for picnics and relaxation.

5. Paget Parish:

Elbow Beach and Grape Bay provide beautiful sections of shoreline for swimming and sunbathing.

Bermuda Botanical Gardens, which displays a diverse range of tropical plants and flowers.

6. Warwick Parish:

Warwick Long Bay is a beautiful beach with delicate pink beaches and crystal blue waves.

Astwood Park is well-known for its stunning cliffside vistas and hiking pathways.

7. Southampton Parish:

Horseshoe Bay Beach, with its unique curving shoreline, is one of Bermuda's most famous beaches.

Gibbs Hill Lighthouse, with sweeping vistas and an insight into maritime history.

8. Sandy's Parish:

The Royal Naval Dockyard is a historic landmark containing museums, shops, restaurants, and the Bermuda National Museum. Somerset Village is well-known for its relaxed environment and proximity to peaceful beaches.

9. St. George's Parish:

The Town of St. George, a UNESCO World Heritage Site, is rich in colonial history and lovely architecture.

Tobacco Bay Beach is a popular snorkelling and underwater marine life exploration destination.

Each parish in Bermuda has a unique combination of natural beauty, historical significance, and cultural richness, giving tourists a wide range of experiences to enjoy throughout their stay.

Must-Visit Attractions In Each Area

Royal Naval Dockyard (Sandys Parish):
Visit the old fortress and the marine museum.
Shopping and eating are available at the Clocktower Mall.
Discover the Dolphin Quest and snorkel at Snorkel Park Beach, which is close.

Horseshoe Bay Beach (Southampton Parish)
Enjoy the famous pink sand and sparkling seas.
Jobson's Cove and Warwick Long Bay are two adjacent coves to see.
Climb Gibbs Hill Lighthouse for spectacular views.

Botanical Gardens (Paget Parish):

Stroll through verdant gardens filled with a variety of plant types.

Camden House and the Masterworks Museum of Bermuda Art are also worth a visit.

Relax on Elbow or Coral Beach.

City of Hamilton (Pembroke Parish):

Shop at the stores and galleries on Front Street.

Discover Bermuda's National Gallery and the Perot Post Office.

Dine and party at a variety of restaurants and pubs.

St. George's Town (St. George's Parish):

Visit UNESCO World Heritage Sites such as St. Peter's Church and St. George's Town Hall.

Investigate Fort St. Catherine and the Deliverance wreckage.

Stroll around the charming streets and visit the local shops and cafés.

Crystal Caves (Hamilton Parish):

Take in the breathtaking crystal formations and subterranean lakes.

For further cave exploring, see Fantasy Cave nearby.

Grotto Bay Beach Resort and Swizzle Inn are two neighbouring attractions.

Bermuda Aquarium, Museum & Zoo (Smith's Parish):

Discover a variety of marine creatures, exhibitions, and educational programmes.

Spittal Pond Nature Reserve is ideal for birding and beautiful hiking.

Relax on the beach at John Smith's Bay.

Somerset Long Bay (Sandys Parish)

Enjoy a less crowded and more tranquil beach experience.

Visit the world's tiniest drawbridge, the ancient Somerset Bridge.

Explore Mangrove Bay and the surrounding area.

Port Royal Golf Course (Southampton Parish):

Play a game of golf while admiring the ocean vistas.

Visit surrounding landmarks such as Church Bay Beach and the Southampton Princess Hotel.

Hidden Gems and Local Favorites

- **Hidden Coves and Beaches:**

Jobson's Cove: This isolated cove, tucked away in South Shore Park, has crystal-clear seas and pink sand, providing a calm respite for beachgoers seeking tranquilly.

Astwood Cove: Nestled among cliffs, Astwood Cove is a lesser-known treasure ideal for snorkelling and watching magnificent sunsets.

- **Off the Beaten Path Historic Sites:**

Fort Scaur: Off the beaten path, this 19th-century bastion provides panoramic views of the Great Sound and is deep in history, yet being frequently neglected by visitors.

Unfinished Church: Located in St. George's Parish, this hauntingly beautiful, partially completed church is an architectural marvel as well as a peaceful place to reflect.

- **Local Eateries and Foodie Discoveries:**

Art Mel's Spicy Dicy: A well-known local food truck known for its spicy fish sandwiches, which provide a real taste of Bermuda.

Woody's Bar and Grill: Woody's, a local favourite, serves traditional Bermudian seafood in a lively, laid-back setting.

- **Parks and nature reserves:**

Cooper's Island Nature Reserve: A hidden jewel for nature lovers, providing walking paths, isolated beaches, and rich birds in a peaceful location.

Spittal Pond Nature Reserve: Bermuda's largest wildlife refuge, with picturesque paths, coastline panoramas, and birding possibilities in tranquil settings.

- **Cultural Experiences Other Than the Main Attractions:**

Bermuda Perfumery: A boutique perfumery that offers tours where tourists may learn how to make perfume using local plants and purchase one-of-a-kind perfumes.

Local Gombey Troupes: Experiencing the bright performances of a Gombey troupe—an vital element of Bermuda's cultural heritage—provides a genuine and colourful experience.

CHAPTER 5: ACTIVITIES AND THINGS TO DO

Beaches And Water Activities

1. Pink-Sand Beaches:

Horseshoe Bay Beach: Famous for its fluffy pink beaches and crystal-clear seas, this renowned beach is ideal for sunbathing, swimming, and snorkelling in the midst of stunning limestone structures.

Elbow Beach: A tranquil stretch of coastline with soft pink beaches and quiet waves, perfect for leisurely strolls and relaxation.

2. Water Activities and Adventures:

Snorkelling and diving: Bermuda's coral reefs, shipwrecks, and marine life make it a snorkelling and diving paradise. Discover diverse underwater environments at Church Bay and Tobacco Bay.

Kayaking and paddleboarding: Bermuda's calm bays and calm seas provide wonderful chances for kayaking and paddleboarding experiences, offering a unique perspective of the shoreline and marine beauties.

Parasailing and Jet Skiing: Thrill-seekers may enjoy jet skiing along the island's coastlines or parasailing over the turquoise waves for magnificent aerial views.

3. Boat Tours and Sailing:

Sunset catamaran cruises or day trips allow tourists to lounge on deck, take up the sun, and discover secret coves and snorkelling sites.

Glass-Bottom Boat excursions: Get a fascinating look of Bermuda's marine life without getting wet on glass-bottom boat excursions, which provide a lively underwater environment without getting wet.

4. Beach Activities for Families:

Castle Island (Shelly Bay Beach): This tiny beach with calm seas is ideal for youngsters to swim and play on. It also has picnic spaces and other attractions.

Tobacco Bay Beach is a family-friendly destination famed for its natural rock formations and small pools teaming with colourful fish—ideal for snorkelling with children.

5. Dining and relaxation on the beach:

Beachfront Restaurants: A variety of beachfront restaurants provide a great eating experience with spectacular ocean views, allowing tourists to savour tasty meals while taking in the coastal environment.

Spa Retreats: Some resorts provide seaside spa services, allowing visitors to rest and enjoy massages while listening to the calming sounds of the ocean.

Adventure Sports And Outdoor Recreation

Consider the salty wind on your face as you zoom over the blue waves, partaking in thrilling water sports. The excitement of speed combined with the panoramic vistas of Bermuda's shoreline offers an amazing adrenaline rush while jet skiing down the coast.

Snorkelling or scuba diving under the waves reveals a secret world of bright marine life and fascinating underwater scenery. Each dive is an adventure filled with colourful corals, lively fish, and the occasional spectacular sea turtle.

Parasailing delivers a bird's-eye perspective of Bermuda's gorgeous shoreline for those looking for airborne vistas and a heart-pounding adventure. The adrenaline thrill of soaring over the cerulean seas while tied to a parachute is unlike any other.

However, the fun doesn't stop at the water's edge. Exploring Bermuda's beautiful scenery and limestone caves provides a unique sense of adventure. Trekking through tropical foliage-adorned pathways, stumbling across secluded coves, or rappelling into strange caverns is an exciting blend of adventure and excitement.

Not to mention the excitement of cliff jumping, which involves a hazardous plunge from the steep cliffs into the tempting turquoise seas below. The exhilaration of freefall, the split-second before the splash, captures the spirit of Bermuda adventure.

The backdrop of Bermuda's natural beauty makes these encounters even more memorable. The combination of craggy beaches, abundant marine life, and lush foliage against the backdrop of the Atlantic Ocean provides a blank canvas for unique adventures.

Cultural Experiences And Tours

Begin your cultural immersion in the Bermuda National Gallery, where the works of local artists and historical artefacts tell the story of Bermuda's legacy. The gallery provides a window into the essence of the island, displaying not just its creative prowess but also its historical growth.

A walk through St. George's, a UNESCO World Heritage Site, is like taking a step back in time. Bermuda's seafaring heritage is conveyed through cobblestone streets, pastel-colored houses, and colonial architecture. Forts like Fort St. Catherine and Fort Hamilton keep vigil over the island's history, providing sweeping vistas and insight into its military history.

Indulge in the island's famed gastronomic pleasures to thoroughly absorb Bermuda's cultural mix. At local restaurants, savour classic meals like fish chowder, Bermuda fish sandwiches, and spiny lobster while enjoying the ocean air. Bermudian cuisine is characterised by a blend of African, British, and Caribbean elements.

Immerse yourself in the rhythmic rhythms of Gombey dancers, who are dressed in colourful costumes and perform traditional Bermudian dance and music. Their contagious enthusiasm and brilliant colours resonate with the island's dynamic spirit.

Take a tour of the Crystal Caves, a natural wonder that seems like something out of a fairytale. These breathtaking underground tunnels studded with stalactites and stalagmites reveal Bermuda's geological wonders, providing a dreamlike experience intermingled with the island's natural beauty.

A visit to the Royal Naval Dockyard gives an insight into Bermuda's maritime history. Explore the historic buildings, craft markets, and the National Museum of Bermuda, where artefacts and interactive exhibitions reveal the island's maritime past.

Engage with locals through various tours and workshops for a more personal cultural experience. Learn about ancient Bermudian crafts like pottery and glassblowing from trained craftsmen who are carrying on these age-old traditions.

3 Days Itinerary

- **Day 1: Exploring Bermuda's History and Natural Environment**

Morning: Begin your day by seeing the Royal Naval Dockyard. Explore historic artefacts and interactive displays at the National Museum of Bermuda to learn about Bermuda's maritime history. Don't miss the beautiful Commissioner's House, which offers panoramic views of the island.

Lunch: At a nearby restaurant, savour regional flavours. Begin your gastronomic adventure with Bermudian fish soup or a typical codfish breakfast.

Afternoon: Visit the breathtaking Crystal Caves, a natural treasure with awe-inspiring crystal formations and an underground lake. Take a guided tour to learn about the geological importance and fascinating history of the cave.

Evening: Take a stroll around St. George's lovely streets as the sun sets. Explore UNESCO-listed ancient monuments such as St. Peter's Church and King's Square. Savour delicious seafood delicacies during a pleasant evening at a cosy restaurant.

- **Beaches and Adventure on Day 2**

Morning: Prepare for a day on the beach at Horseshoe Bay Beach. Sink your toes into the pink dunes and swim in the pristine waters. Don't forget to check out the adjacent coves for peaceful areas and great snorkelling.

Lunch: Recharge with a seaside picnic or dine at a local café, where you may enjoy Bermudian cuisine while overlooking the ocean.

Afternoon: Water sports such as paddleboarding or kayaking along the shore are ideal for thrill seekers. Visit the Bermuda Aquarium, Museum, and Zoo to learn about the island's rich marine life and wildlife conservation activities.

Evening: Enjoy a sunset cruise while drinking a nice drink and seeing Bermuda's shoreline from the ocean. Finish your day with a delicious meal at a beachfront restaurant, where you can sample fresh catch-of-the-day cuisine.

- **Day 3: Relaxation and Culture**

Morning: Begin your day by visiting the Bermuda Botanical Gardens. Explore lush scenery, colourful blossoms, and peaceful locations, ideal for a morning stroll.

Lunch: Enjoy a peaceful spa treatment at one of Bermuda's luxury resorts or a leisurely lunch at a gorgeous garden café.

Afternoon: Explore Hamilton's historic district. Visit the Bermuda National Gallery to see local art or meander down Front Street to see attractive boutiques and shops.

Evening: As the day comes to an end, treat yourself to a goodbye meal at a fine dining establishment, where you may indulge in gourmet food and perhaps taste Bermuda's famed rum-infused sweets.

7 Days Itinerary

Day 1: Arrival and Exploration of Hamilton

Arrive in Bermuda in the morning and check into your hotel.

Afternoon: Travel to Hamilton, the lively capital. Explore the colourful boutiques on Front Street, eat at a local restaurant, and take in some art and culture at the Bermuda National Gallery.

Evening: Enjoy a leisurely meal with a view of Hamilton Harbour.

Day 2: Horseshoe Bay Beach and Gibbs Hill Lighthouse

Morning: Begin your day at the beautiful Horseshoe Bay Beach. Bathe in the pink beaches, swim in the crystal-clear waters, and take in the stunning environment.

Afternoon: Head to the neighbouring Gibbs Hill Lighthouse for panoramic views of the island.

Evening: At a seaside restaurant, sample Bermuda's seafood delicacies.

Day 3: Exploration of St. George's and Tobacco Bay

Travel to St. George's, a UNESCO World Heritage Site, in the morning. Explore the picturesque streets, St. Peter's Church, and historical sights including St. Catherine's Fort.

Afternoon: Go snorkelling or sunbathing at Tobacco Bay Beach.

Evening: Savour local food over a meal in St. George's.

Day 4: Visit Somerset Village and the Dockyard

In the morning, take the boat to Somerset Village. Explore the neighbourhood and see sites such as Somerset Bridge, the world's smallest drawbridge, and the serene Mangrove Bay.

In the afternoon, visit the Royal Naval Dockyard. Explore the National Museum of Bermuda, the artisan markets, and the dockyard's perimeter to watch the sunset.

Evening: Return to your starting point and dine at a restaurant with beautiful views.

Day 5: Spittal Pond and Crystal Caves Nature Day

Visit Spittal Pond Nature Reserve in the morning for birds and picturesque pathways.

Afternoon: Explore the enthralling Crystal Caves. Admire the beautiful structures and crystal-clear waterways.

Evening: Have supper at a cosy restaurant near your hotel.

Day 6: Hamilton Cultural Day and Museums

Return to Hamilton in the morning for a more in-depth exploration. Visit historical sites such as Fort Hamilton and buy goods at local markets.

Afternoon: Visit the Bermuda Underwater Exploration Institute or the Historical Society Museum to learn about Bermuda's history.

Evening: In Hamilton, treat yourself to a superb dinner experience.

Day 7: Rest and Departure

Morning: Enjoy a peaceful morning at a local beach or go on a nature walk to soak up the tranquilly of the island.

Afternoon: Check out of your hotel and have a goodbye meal at a beach restaurant.

Evening: Leave Bermuda with fond memories.

CHAPTER 6: DINING AND CUISINE IN BERMUDA

Bermudian Cuisine Overview

Fish Chowder: A traditional Bermudian dish, fish chowder is a substantial soup made with fish stock, tomatoes, onions, peppers, and a variety of spices including sherry pepper sauce and Gosling's Black Seal Rum. This meal is a real flavour of Bermuda, served with a side of Outerbridge's Sherry Peppers sauce.

Codfish Breakfast: Codfish paired with potatoes, boiled egg, banana, avocado, and a savoury sauce is a popular breakfast option. This traditional meal illustrates the island's affinity for the sea and its flavours.

Cassava Pie: A delectable pie made from cassava, a root vegetable related to yucca. This savoury meal, made with spices, butter, and occasionally meat, is a local and visitor favourite.

Hoppin' John: This meal is influenced by African cuisine and consists of rice, black-eyed peas, and salty pork. The blend of flavours and textures makes it a flavorful and pleasant option.

Bermuda Fish Sandwich: Served on raisin bread or a bun, this sandwich is made with crispy fried fish fillets, coleslaw, tartar sauce and sometimes a piece of Bermuda onion. It's a wonderful and satisfying meal that's popular in local restaurants.

Rum Cake: No trip to Bermuda is complete without sampling the island's famous rum cake.

This delectable dessert, made with local Gosling's Black Seal Rum, is moist, flavorful, and frequently a treasured gift to take home.

Dark 'n Stormy: While not technically a cuisine, this legendary Bermuda drink created with Gosling's Black Seal Rum and ginger beer is a must-try. It nicely compliments the food and culture of the island.

Top Restaurants And Local Eateries

Marcus': This restaurant, founded by famous chef Marcus Samuelsson, mixes Bermudian ingredients with Samuelsson's unique flair, serving inventive dishes like as shellfish bouillabaisse and jerk pig belly.

The Waterlot Inn: This restaurant is nestled amid the historic surroundings of the 350-year-old Southampton Princess. Enjoy well prepared steaks, fresh seafood, and a comprehensive wine selection while overlooking the harbour.

The Swizzle Inn: A popular neighbourhood hangout known for its relaxed environment and outstanding rum swizzles. In a relaxed atmosphere, enjoy Bermudian favourites including fish sandwiches, fish chowder, and hearty pub cuisine.

Art Mel's Spicy Dicey: This food truck serves you wonderful fish sandwiches and spicy fish cakes with authentic Bermudian flavours. It's a local and visitor favourite for its inexpensive, tasty fare.

Mad Hatters: Mad Hatters is a fascinating dining experience recognised for its eccentric décor and inventive food. In a delightful setting, dishes like lobster ravioli and duck breast highlight a combination of flavours.

The Lobster Pot: This seafood restaurant on the water's edge in Hamilton is noted for its fresh lobster meals, fish specialties, and spectacular harbour views.

Devil's Isle: A hip café and restaurant that serves farm-to-table cuisine. From brunch to evening, their cuisine incorporates locally sourced ingredients into delectable meals such as coconut curry mussels and innovative salads.

Woody's Sports Bar is a popular neighbourhood hangout for Bermudian fish sandwiches and a vibrant environment. It's a terrific spot to meet locals while eating delicious, no-fuss meals.

Dining Etiquette And Tips

Reservations are recommended, especially at famous restaurants or during busy tourist seasons. This guarantees you a table and cuts down on waiting time.

Dress Code: Many restaurants in Bermuda, particularly upmarket venues, have a dress code. Check ahead of time to ensure that you are dressed appropriately, which may include business casual or resort wear.

Punctuality: It is nice to be on time for your reservation. Being timely demonstrates respect for the restaurant's timetable and other diners in Bermudian culture.

Tipping is prevalent in Bermuda and often runs from 15% to 20% of the entire cost. Some restaurants may impose a service charge, so double-check your receipt before giving an extra tip.

Table Manners: Proper use of utensils and napkins, as well as courteous conversation, contribute to a nice meal experience. Before beginning your meal, keep your elbows off the table and wait for everyone to be served.

Local customs include tasting Bermudian dishes and recognising cultural differences. Engaging with locals and soliciting advice might enrich your eating experience.

Special food Needs: Let the server know if you have any food restrictions or allergies. Most eateries in Bermuda are friendly and will try their utmost to accommodate your demands.

Patience: Take your time and appreciate the relaxed pace of Bermudian eating. Meals are frequently a social event and may take longer than in other cultures. Enjoy your dinner and the folks you're with throughout this time.

Cell Phones: To demonstrate concern for others, keep phone usage to a minimum or to emergencies only. Engage with your dinner friends and enjoy the atmosphere.

CHAPTER 7: SHOPPING IN BERMUDA

Souvenirs And Local Crafts

Imagine yourself wandering around Hamilton or visiting the charming streets of St. George, surrounded by a variety of colourful, locally created artefacts that capture the soul of Bermuda.

Let's begin with the classic Bermuda shorts. These aren't just ordinary shorts; they represent the island's history and flair. They're a must-have keepsake for anybody visiting, and come in a variety of colourful colours and patterns. You may get them in specialist shops or at local craftsmen' markets, and each pair has a distinct Bermuda flair.

Bermuda, when it comes to the craft scene, has wonderful handmade objects that represent its rich history and cultural variety. The famed hand-woven products on the island, such as the sweet-grass baskets, are truly pieces of art. These baskets, made using ancient skills passed down through generations, are both utilitarian and physically appealing, making them a wonderful remembrance or present.

Don't miss out on exploring the Bermuda Craft Market in Dockyard, a treasure trove of locally crafted products. There's plenty for everyone, from elaborate jewellery items embellished with

Bermuda's trademark pink sand to ceramics, woodwork, and hand-painted artworks.

Furthermore, in their paintings and sculptures, local artists frequently depict the island's stunning vistas and active life. Their masterpieces, which portray Bermuda's gorgeous seascapes or the island's flora and animals, are an excellent way to take a bit of the island's beauty home with you.

And don't forget about the amazing gastronomic treats! Locally created jams, sauces, and rum cakes are not only wonderful, but also make excellent gifts for friends and family who want to sample Bermuda's flavours.

So, when in Bermuda, visit the local craft markets, talk to the craftspeople, and find these gems that capture the character of the island. Each item has a story to tell, a slice of

Bermuda's character, making them more than just souvenirs, but treasured keepsakes of your Bermuda adventure.

Shopping Districts And Markets

A stroll down Front Street in Hamilton, the capital, reveals a treasure trove of shops, galleries and specialised businesses. The colonial architecture in this area provides a timeless charm to the shopping experience. Everything from high-end apparel and jewellery to locally produced gifts that eloquently capture Bermuda's culture and tradition may be found here.

Exploring St. George's lovely town is like going back in time. Its cobblestone alleys are packed with artisanal stores and craft fairs where creative residents sell their handcrafted wares. The historic environment enhances the shopping experience, making it a must-see for anyone looking for real Bermudian wares.

Don't miss the island's lively markets, which provide a delectable mix of fresh vegetables, handcrafted crafts, and local delicacies. The Bermuda Farmer's Market is a foodie's delight, featuring a plethora of farm-fresh fruits, veggies, and exquisite sweets that showcase the island's culinary skill.

Not to mention the bustling street vendors and pop-up stalls that provide an unusual variety of things. From brightly coloured handmade fabrics to one-of-a-kind artwork and jewellery, these local merchants inject a sense of spontaneity and authenticity into the shopping experience.

What actually distinguishes Bermuda's retail areas and marketplaces is the inhabitants' warm warmth and genuine zeal. Their delight in their work and readiness to tell tales about it make buying here more than simply a transaction—it's an opportunity to connect with Bermuda's heart and soul.

Best Deals And Bargaining Tips

Local Markets and Vendors: Visit the vibrant local markets such as the Dockyard Craft Market and the Hamilton Farmers' Market. These locations are ideal for discovering one-of-a-kind handcrafted products, artwork, and local items. Engage with sellers, express interest in their products, and you may be able to negotiate pricing, especially if you are purchasing numerous things.

Off-Season Shopping: It's all about timing! Consider going during the off-season (usually November to March), when hotels, restaurants, and stores may offer cheaper pricing or special promotions to entice travellers during slower times.

While bargaining isn't as frequent in Bermuda as it is elsewhere, there's no harm in respectfully negotiating, especially at markets or smaller businesses. Respectful negotiating with a smile and a nice demeanour can occasionally result in reductions or other advantages.

Local Suggestions: Talk to the locals! They frequently have intimate knowledge of where to discover the greatest prices or lesser-known locations that provide better value. Start discussions at cafés, pubs, or on excursions to gain vital insights.

Package bargains: Look for packaged bargains or packages offered by travel operators or excursion businesses. These might include discounts on activities such as snorkelling expeditions, island tours, or even transportation, which can help you save money on specific purchases.

Coupons and Loyalty Programmes: Some retailers and companies may have loyalty programmes or give coupons in local periodicals or online. Use these to gain access to additional savings or benefits throughout your stay.

Ask for Discounts: Don't be hesitant to ask for discounts, especially if you're a student, elderly citizen, or a member of any other special organisations that may be eligible for lower rates. A little courtesy goes a long way!

CHAPTER 8: NIGHTLIFE AND ENTERTAINMENT

Bars, Pubs, And Nightclubs

Bermuda has a varied variety of bars, each with its own distinct vibe and amenities. There's something for everyone, from cosy, traditional pubs to fashionable cocktail lounges. Waterfront bars are the places to go if you want to relax and have a drink while gazing out at the ocean. Some bars also have live music, which adds to the lively environment and makes for a unique experience.

Bermuda's pubs are a sanctuary for people looking for a more casual and genuine environment. These places frequently radiate a cosy, local vibe, making them ideal for unwinding after a day of exploring. You'll discover a variety of locally made beers and frequently the opportunity to connect with friendly locals or fellow travellers, which makes for wonderful talks and unforgettable memories.

Bermuda's nightclubs come up to the plate when the night calls for dancing and letting free. These places usually have bustling atmospheres, lively music, and dynamic crowds. You may dance to a combination of worldwide and local hits, creating an exhilarating atmosphere that keeps the excitement high into the early hours.

Live Music And Performances

Bermuda's native music industry is broad and deep, featuring a combination of traditional sounds and current beats that reflect the island's distinct culture.

Imagine yourself wandering through Bermuda's lovely neighbourhoods or relaxing on one of its beautiful beaches while the air becomes alive with the irresistible rhythm of live music. The island features an eclectic blend of musical styles that represent its diverse background, ranging from deep reggae melodies to the explosive sounds of calypso and steel pan ensembles.

The pulse of live performances fills the island's venues, whether seaside bars, cosy taverns, or bustling clubs. You may come across outstanding local bands performing at attractive waterfront places such as Hamilton's Front Street or small pubs in St. George's, creating an atmosphere that inspires you to immerse yourself in the music and join the rhythm.

Keep an eye out for unique events or music festivals that appear on Bermuda's calendar. These events include both local and international musicians, providing an unprecedented opportunity to hear a fusion of songs set against Bermuda's magnificent settings.

Not to mention the cultural performances! Bermuda's cultural acts range from traditional Gombey dancers in colourful costumes parading through the streets to theatrical shows commemorating the island's history and culture. They are a monument to the island's rich past and inventiveness.

Evening Events And Festivals

As the sun sets over this enthralling island, a tapestry of nighttime activities and festivals develops, providing tourists with a pleasant experience.

Consider yourself in the thick of the vivid energy of Harbour Nights, a legendary monthly event in Hamilton, the capital. Colourful merchants, local artists, and superb musicians fill the streets, creating a captivating environment. You'll be enveloped in a kaleidoscope of sights and sounds, with jewellery gleaming beneath the warm glow of lamps, the perfume of wonderful island food wafting through the air, and the melodious rhythms of steel pan drums filling the night.

Prepare for a sensory overload if you visit during one of Bermuda's festivals, such as the

Bermuda Festival of the Performing Arts or Bermuda Heroes Weekend. The island vibrates with music, dance, and dramatic acts that highlight Bermuda's and its people's rich cultural past. Each event weaves a beautiful tale of history and celebration, whether it's the rhythmic beats of Gombey dancers marching through the streets or the stunning performances at the Bermuda Arts Centre.

A sunset drink cruise around the shore provides a more intimate experience. As you sip your favourite drink while soaking in the golden hues of the setting sun painting the sky, the calm waves of the Atlantic Ocean create a soothing backdrop.

Not to mention the wonderful glowworm cruises! On a warm evening, go outside to see nature's stunning light show, in which innumerable bioluminescent glowworms illuminate the water, producing a mesmerising spectacle right out of a fairy tale.

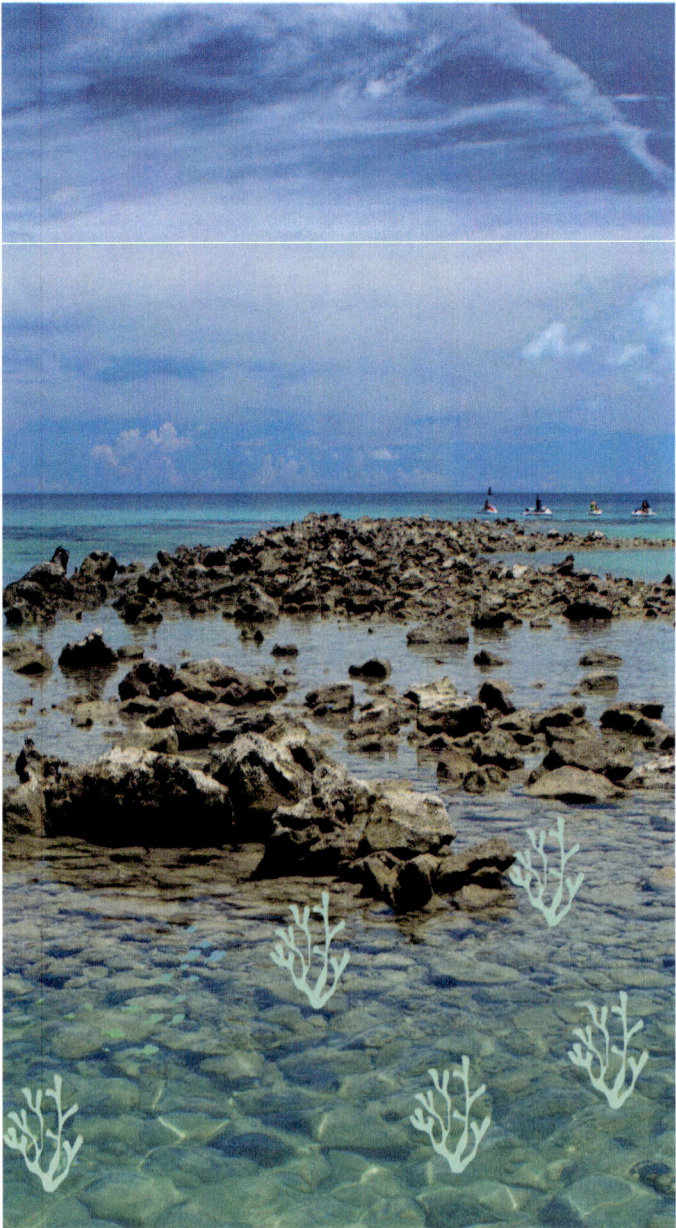

CHAPTER 9: PRACTICAL TRAVEL TIPS

Currency And Money Matters

The Bermudian dollar (BMD) is the national currency, and it is pegged to the US dollar at a 1:1 ratio. This implies that the two currencies are interchangeable, and both US and Bermudan dollars are commonly accepted across the island.

When it comes to money, credit and debit cards are widely accepted in Bermuda, particularly in tourist areas, hotels, and restaurants. However, having extra cash on hand is a smart idea for smaller places and local markets where card acceptance may be limited.

Now, onto Bermuda's financial allure! Because of its favourable tax structure and powerful regulatory framework, the island occupies a key place in international finance. It is a global hub for reinsurance and insurance-linked products, attracting businesses looking for a stable and attractive business climate.

Another feature is the Bermuda Stock Exchange (BSX), which provides a venue for listing a range of products, including shares, funds, and insurance-linked instruments. This trade helps to facilitate international financial flows and investment possibilities.

Bermuda's financial scene also features a strong presence of offshore banking and investment services, making it an appealing location for anyone looking for wealth management solutions or offshore company formation.

Safety And Health Information

Medical Services: Although Bermuda has outstanding medical facilities, it is critical to carry travel insurance that covers healthcare and emergencies. In case of an emergency, familiarise yourself with the locations of hospitals, clinics, and pharmacies.

Sun Protection: The sun can be fairly harsh in Bermuda, so bring sunscreen, hats, and sunglasses to protect yourself from sunburn and other heat-related ailments. Hydration is critical, especially while participating in outdoor activities.

Water Safety: Although Bermuda has beautiful beaches, some spots may have strong currents. Pay heed to warning signs, and if you're not a skilled swimmer, limit your swimming to approved zones. Always keep an eye on youngsters who are near water.

Precautions for Insects: While not a huge problem, it's a good idea to apply insect repellent, especially in more forested or grassy regions, to avoid mosquito bites.

Food and Water Safety: Bermuda has generally good food and water safety regulations. However, it is still recommended to consume bottled or boiled water and to practise good food hygiene, especially in local restaurants.

Save emergency numbers such as the local police, ambulance, and your country's embassy or consulate in case you require quick assistance.

Environmental Concerns: Bermuda is noted for its beautiful landscapes and diverse flora and wildlife. When touring natural reserves or parks, respect the environment by not disturbing wildlife, avoiding littering, and staying on approved pathways.

Traffic Safety: If you want to hire a scooter or drive, keep in mind that Bermuda drives on the left side of the road. Maintain vigilance, obey speed restrictions, and wear helmets whenever riding a scooter.

Finally, remember to apply common sense and trust your intuition. It's alright to take a step back or seek help if something doesn't seem secure or comfortable.

Communication And Connectivity

Communication:

Communication is an art form in Bermuda that combines history and contemporary. While English is the official language, interactions are enhanced by the local Bermudian accent, a rhythmic combination of English, Portuguese, and West African elements. Engaging with people in their colloquial language may be a fun way to learn about the island's rich history.

Communication flourishes via amicable encounters, whether you're meandering through the colourful streets of Hamilton, the capital city, or sunbathing on the pink sand beaches. Conversations with friendly residents provide insights into Bermuda's history, traditions, and thriving community life.

Connectivity:

Despite its tranquil atmosphere, Bermuda is well-connected, with strong communication infrastructure. Internet access is generally available, letting guests to keep connected with the rest of the world while relaxing on the island's tranquilly. Staying connected is simple, thanks to high-speed Wi-Fi at hotels and cafés and dependable cell networks.

Exploring Bermuda's stunning scenery does not imply completely unplugging. Indeed, technology frequently improves the experience by offering access to navigation aids, educational applications about local sites, and chances to share the beauty of Bermuda's surroundings with friends and family all over the world.

Furthermore, the connectedness on the island goes beyond the digital domain. Engaging with nature and the local people, whether by snorkelling in crystal-clear seas, discovering ancient sights like St. George's Town, or just savouring real Bermudian food at local cafés, builds a deeper connection. These encounters foster long-lasting bonds with the island and its people, moving beyond basic connectedness to a more profound understanding of Bermuda's allure.

CHAPTER 10: SUSTAINABILITY AND RESPONSIBLE TRAVEL

Environmental Conservation Efforts

Beach Cleanups: Organise or participate in beach cleanups. The beautiful beaches are frequently ruined by plastic garbage and litter. Gather a group of travellers or residents and commit a day to cleaning the beaches, safeguarding marine life, and maintaining the beautiful splendour.

Bermuda has beautiful coral reefs that must be preserved. Volunteer with local organisations to help with reef conservation efforts. Contribute to reef health monitoring, coral planting, or educational programmes to raise awareness about reef conservation.

Removal of Invasive Species: Invasive species pose a threat to Bermuda's unique ecology. Join conservation organisations in eradicating invasive plants and animals to protect native flora and fauna. This hands-on initiative has the potential to have a big influence on the island's biodiversity.

Trash Reduction activities: Encourage trash reduction and recycling activities. Encourage businesses to implement eco-friendly practises and decrease the usage of single-use plastics. Attend educational sessions to discover how to reduce your personal environmental impact.

Advocating for Sustainable Tourism Practises: Advocate for sustainable tourism practises. Select eco-friendly lodging, engage in nature-friendly activities, and patronise local companies that prioritise environmental protection.

Participate in educational outreach programmes, especially if you're visiting with children. Encourage young minds to respect and conserve the environment, building a conservation-minded future generation.

Encourage and put into practise energy conservation strategies. Reduce carbon emissions by taking public transit, walking or cycling around the island. Respect local energy and water conservation rules.

Donate to or volunteer for local conservation organisations that are actively trying to preserve Bermuda's environment. Both financial assistance and hands-on engagement have an equal impact.

Responsible Tourism Practices

Environment Protection: Bermuda's natural beauty is its treasure. Reduce your usage of plastic, recycle, and properly dispose of rubbish to practise responsible waste management. To safeguard fragile ecosystems, take part in beach clean-ups and hike authorised pathways.

Respecting Marine Life: Prioritise appropriate diving and snorkelling practises whilst exploring Bermuda's magnificent waters. Never touch or disturb marine animals, and never take shells or coral. Select eco-friendly water activities that contribute to conservation efforts.

Supporting Local Culture: Engage in Bermuda's rich cultural legacy with respect. Discover the history, traditions, and customs of the island. Purchase original crafts and souvenirs rather than mass-produced things to support local craftspeople.

Choosing Eco-Friendly Hotels or Lodges: Look for eco-friendly hotels or lodges that prioritise sustainability. Look for businesses that are devoted to lowering energy use, successfully managing waste, and helping local communities.

Explore local cuisine and patronise eateries that provide food that is responsibly sourced.

Choose restaurants that utilise locally grown vegetables and support food waste reduction projects.

Responsible transit: Instead of renting a car, consider taking public transit, biking, or walking to tour the island. Choose eco-friendly transportation to reduce your carbon footprint.

Respecting Local Communities: Interact with locals respectfully by learning about their practises and welcoming them courteously. Keep in mind local legislation, customs, and traditions, and make sure your behaviour matches their expectations.

Educate and Raise Awareness: Tell people about your experiences with responsible tourism in Bermuda. Encourage fellow visitors to make mindful decisions when visiting the island by advocating for sustainable practises.

Ways To Support Local Communities

Local Markets: Visit local markets such as the Bermuda Craft Market or the Historic Town of St. George's. Purchasing locally manufactured crafts, artwork, or items helps craftsmen and small businesses directly.

Eat at Local Restaurants: Choose restaurants and food booths that provide authentic Bermudian cuisine. While supporting local chefs and businesses, enjoy meals like fish chowder, fish sandwiches, or cassava pie.

Choose Local Tours and Services: Instead of major chain tour firms, look for local guides or tour businesses. This not only delivers a more realistic experience, but it also helps those who understand and respect Bermuda's culture.

Visit Cultural Attractions: Museums, historic sites, and cultural centres may all help to preserve local history. Your visit contributes to the preservation of these important pieces of Bermuda's heritage.

Participate in Local Art and Music: Go to art exhibits, live music concerts, or performances that include Bermudian talent. Buying artwork or going to concerts directly benefits local artists and musicians.

Bermuda's natural beauty is a treasure, so please respect it. Participate in beach clean-ups or select environmentally friendly activities that encourage sustainability. Supporting environmental projects helps to maintain the island's allure for future generations.

Stay at Local Accommodations: Instead of foreign chains, choose locally owned hotels, guesthouses, or bed & breakfasts. Your visit directly benefits the livelihoods of Bermudian business owners and employees.

Consider volunteering or donating your time to local charities or organisations if you have the time. Donating to organisations that assist education, healthcare, or community development can have a long-term good influence.

Engage with the people, ask questions, and learn about Bermuda's history, culture, and traditions. Respect and admiration for the local culture go a long way towards ensuring its survival.

Spread the Word: Share your experiences on social media or in reviews, emphasising the significance of supporting Bermuda's local communities. Encourage others to follow suit when they come to visit.

Fort St. Catherine
The St. Regis Bermuda Resort
Barry Rd
Fort Victoria, Bermuda
Secretary Rd
Unfinished Church
Drew's Bay
St George's
St.George's
York St
Queen St
Cruise Ship Terminal
St. George's Ferry Terminal
St. George's Island
Alexandra Battery
Gates Fort
St. George's Dinghy & Sports Club
Higgs and Horseshoe Island
Paget Island
Hen Island
Peggy's Island
Whalers Islands
Smith's Island
Governor's Island, Bermuda
Burt's Island
Brooks Island, Bermuda
Hideaway Farms
St George's Harbour
St George's Channel
Smith's Sound
Banjo Island
Stokes Point Nature Reserve
Schultz Isle
Xtreme Sports Fun Zone
Strykz Bowling Lounge
Double Dip Express
Bermuda Institute of Ocean Sciences
RUBIS Energy Bermuda
Oil Docks
Co-Educational Facility
Ferry Reach
Railway Trail
Echo Ln
Southside Road
Carter House
St. David's Seafood & Grill
Fort Popple

108

Admiral's Cave
Admiralty House Park
SPANISH POINT
Deep Bay Beach
Mouse Island
Hinson's Island
Partridge Island
Bird Island, Bermuda
Agar's Island
Point Shares
Bluck's Island
Watling Island
Hinson's Island Ferry
ESC Limited
Point Mart
Price Rite Pembroke Bermuda
The Berkeley Institute
N Shore Rd
Gorham's Ltd
Saltus Island
Spectacle Island
Reid Island
Doctors Island
Salt Kettle Ferry
Darrell's Wharf
Hamilton Princess & Beach Club - A...
Hamilton Bermuda
Royal Palms
Pitts Bay Rd
Berkeley Rd
Bull's Head Car Park
Miles Market Ltd
Victoria Park
Devil's Isle Cafe
Hamilton
Hamilton Harbour, Bermuda
Spa Oasis
Bermuda Transport Control Department
St. Theresa's Catholic Cathedral
Marsh Folly Composting Facility
Art Mel's Spicy Dicy
House of India
Ruby Murray's
Latte's coffee & pastry
Newstead Belmont Hills Golf Resort and Spa
Lower Ferry
Royal Hamilton Amateur Dinghy Club
The Supermart
Centre @ Bermuda
Ocean Discovery
Autobahn Accessories
NORTHSHORE Medical & Aesthetics Center
North Shore Village
PEMBROKE PARISH
DEVONSHIRE PARISH
Scooter Mart
Ice Queen
Oleander Cycles - Headquarters
Modern Mart
Grape Bay Cottages
Devonshire Dock
Cedarbridge Academy
Bermuda National Sports Centre
Prospect Police Recreation Club
Arboretum
Consulate General of the United States
Camden
Lewi Ackerman's Tea Shop
Bermuda Botanical Gardens
South Rd
Middle Rd
Tynes Bay Waste to Energy Facility
Bermuda Waterworks Limited
Amaral Farms
Cedar Tree Vets
Hungry Bay Nature Reserve

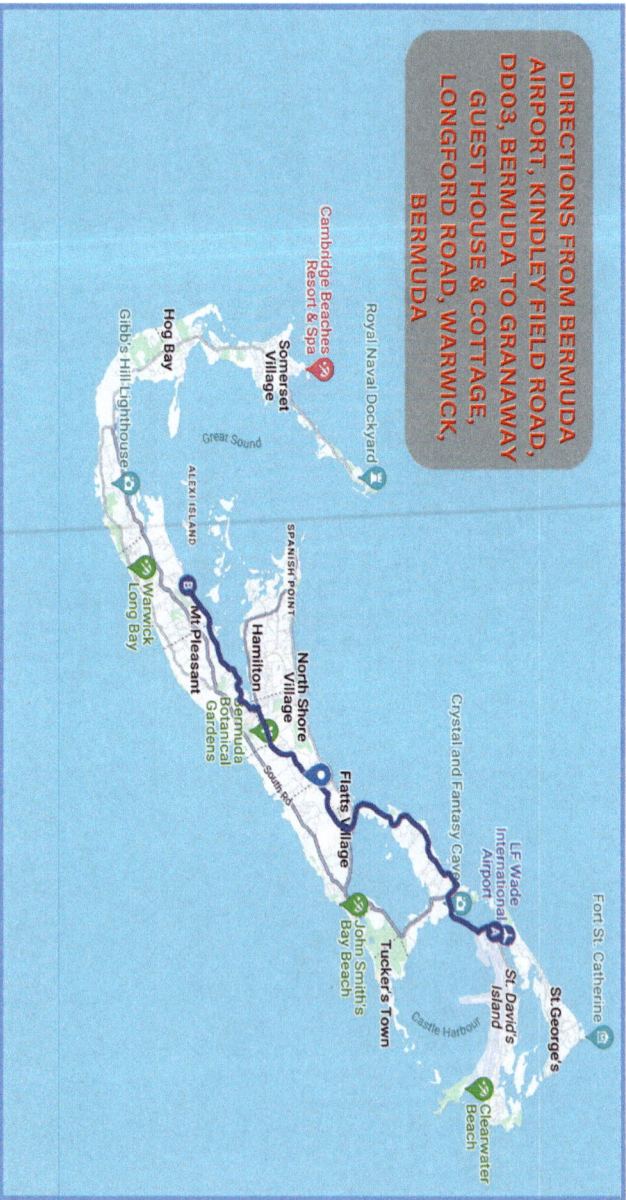

DIRECTIONS FROM BERMUDA AIRPORT, KINDLEY FIELD ROAD, DD03, BERMUDA TO GRANAWAY GUEST HOUSE & COTTAGE, LONGFORD ROAD, WARWICK, BERMUDA

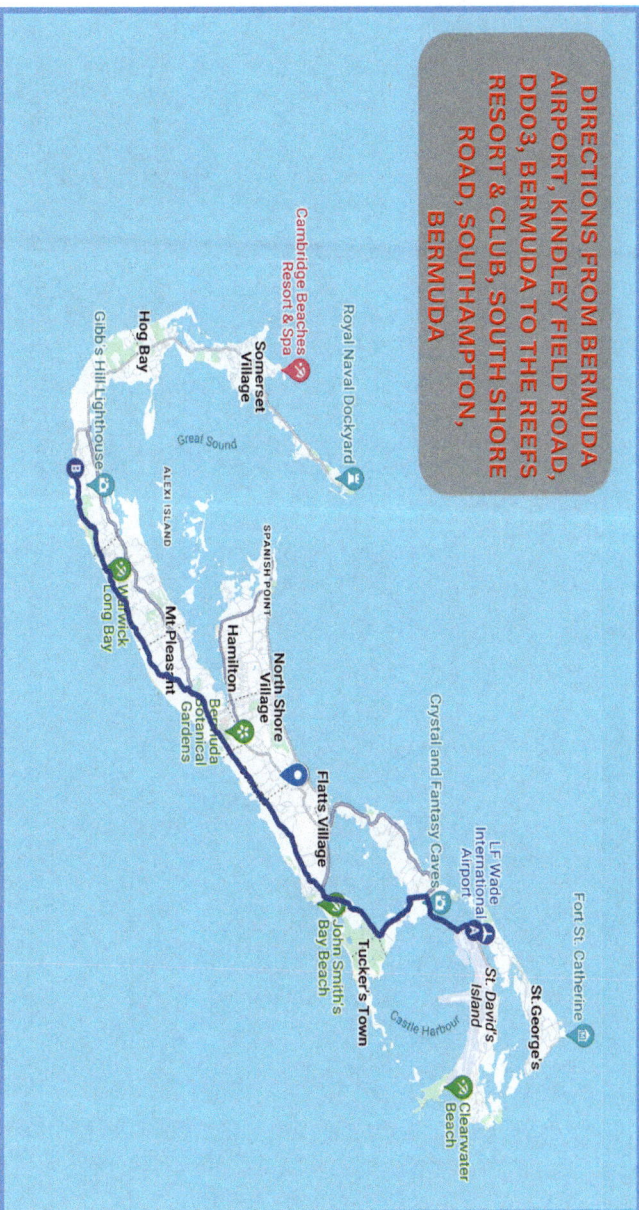

DIRECTIONS FROM BERMUDA AIRPORT, KINDLEY FIELD ROAD, DD03, BERMUDA TO THE REEFS RESORT & CLUB, SOUTH SHORE ROAD, SOUTHAMPTON, BERMUDA

Cambridge Beaches Resort & Spa

Royal Naval Dockyard

Somerset Village

Hog Bay

Gibb's Hill Lighthouse

Great Sound

ALEXI ISLAND

SPANISH POINT

Warwick Long Bay

Mt. Pleasant

Hamilton

Bermuda Botanical Gardens

North Shore Village

Flatts Village

Crystal and Fantasy Caves

L.F. Wade International Airport

John Smith's Bay Beach

Tucker's Town

Castle Harbour

St. David's Island

Fort St. Catherine

St. George's

Cleawater Beach

111

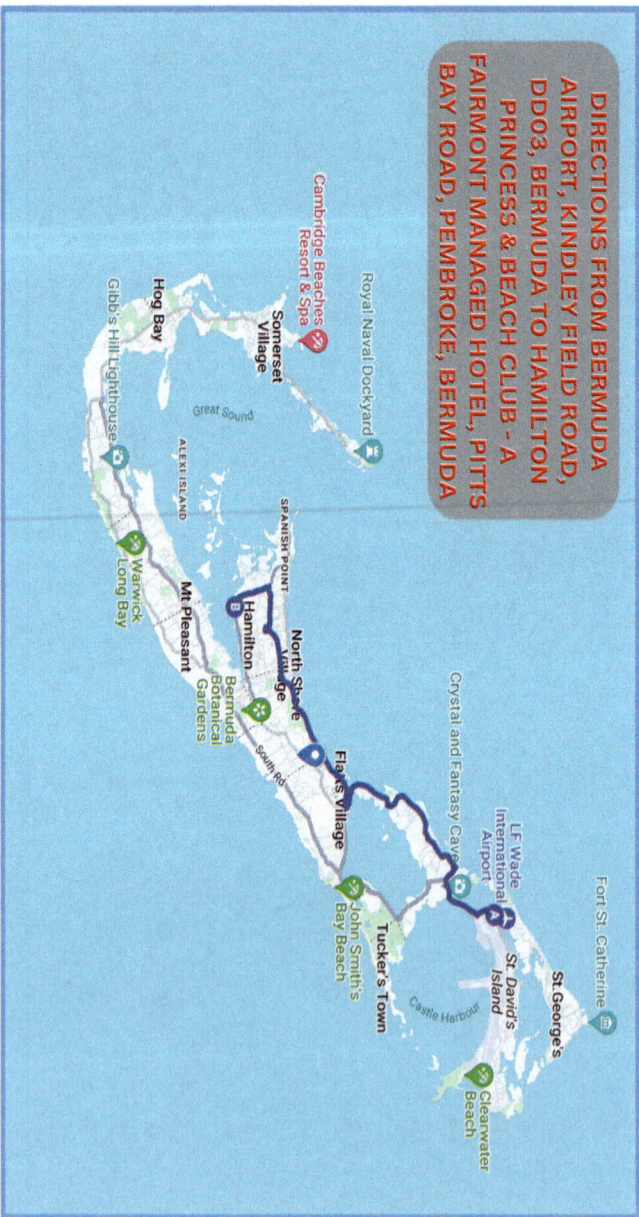

DIRECTIONS FROM BERMUDA AIRPORT, KINDLEY FIELD ROAD, DD03, BERMUDA TO HAMILTON PRINCESS & BEACH CLUB - A FAIRMONT MANAGED HOTEL, PITTS BAY ROAD, PEMBROKE, BERMUDA

Printed in Great Britain
by Amazon

43285892R00066